LOW-CARB RECIPES

Hors D'oeuvres – Snacks – Party Nibbles

The Complete Guide with 50+ Simple and Yummy Low-Carb Recipes to Impress Your Friends And Family

Introduction

Occasional snacks can be fun. Festive. Crunchy! Make them low carb with these tasty recipes. Maybe you seek melt-in-your-mouth cheese puffs, chips, and dips, crispy onion rings, or a quick keto latte? Look no further for healthy options, snacking has never been this delicious!

—

Heroin Wings

Once you try these, you'll understand the name-they're utterly, totally addictive! These are a bit messy and time-consuming to make, but they're worth every minute. They'll impress the heck out of your friends, too, and you'll wish you'd made more of them. They also taste great the next day.

4 pounds chicken wings
1 cup grated Parmesan cheese 2 tablespoons dried parsley
1 tablespoon dried oregano
2 teaspoons paprika
1 teaspoon salt
1/2 teaspoon pepper
1/2 cup butter

1. Preheat the oven to 350°F.

2. Cut the wings into drumsticks, saving the pointy tips.

   Not sure what to do with those wingtips? Freeze them for soup -they make great broth.

3. Combine the Parmesan cheese and the parsley, oregano, paprika, salt, and pepper in a bowl.

4. Line a shallow baking pan with foil. (Do not omit this step, or you'll still be scrub- bing the pan a week later.)

5. Melt the butter in a shallow bowl or pan.

6. Dip each drumstick in butter, roll in the cheese and seasoning mixture, and arrange in the foil-lined pan.

7. Bake for 1 hour,-and then kick yourself for not having made a double recipe!

Yield: About 50 pieces, each with only a trace of carbohydrates, a trace of fiber, and 4 grams of protein.

—

Chinese Peanut Wings

If you love Chinese barbecued spareribs, try making these.

1/4 cup soy sauce
3 tablespoons Splenda
3 tablespoons natural peanut butter
2 tablespoons dry sherry
1 tablespoon oil
1 tablespoon apple cider vinegar
2 teaspoons Chinese Five Spice powder
1/4 teaspoon red pepper flakes (or more, if you want them hotter) 1 clove garlic, crushed
12 chicken wings or 24 drumettes

1. Preheat the oven to 325°.

2. Put the soy sauce, Splenda, peanut butter, sherry, oil, vinegar, spice powder,

    pepper flakes, and garlic in a blender or food processor, and blend well.

3. If you have whole chicken wings and want to cut them into drumsticks, do it now. (This is a matter of preference and is not essential.)

4. Arrange the wings in a large baking pan, and pour the blended sauce over them, then turn them over to coat on all sides.

5. Let them sit for at least half an hour (an hour is even better).

6. Bake the wings for an hour, turning every 20 minutes during baking.

7. When the wings are done, put them on a serving platter and scrape the sauce from the pan back into the blender or food processor. Blend again for just a moment to

make it smooth, and serve with the wings.

Yield: 24 pieces, each with 1 gram of carbohydrates, a trace of fiber, and 5 grams of protein.

Hot Wings

If you want to simplify this recipe, use store-bought Buffalo Wing sauce instead of the mixture of dry spices. Most wing sauces don't have any sugar in them and are quite low in carbs.

1 teaspoon cayenne pepper 2 teaspoons dried oregano 1 teaspoon curry powder
2 teaspoons paprika

2 teaspoons dried thyme
2 pounds chicken wings, cut into drumettes

1. Preheat the oven to 375°F.
2. Combine the pepper, oregano, curry, paprika, and thyme well in a bowl.

Arrange the wings in a shallow baking pan, and sprinkle the mixture evenly over them, turning to coat both sides.

Roast for 45 to 50 minutes, or until crisp. Serve with the traditional accompaniments of ranch or blue cheese dressing and celery sticks, if desired.

Yield: About 24 pieces, each with a trace of carbohydrates, a trace of fiber, and 4 grams of protein.

Paprika Wings

20 chicken wing drumsticks 3 tablespoons olive oil
2 cloves garlic, crushed
Salt

Pepper Paprika

1. Preheat the oven to 350°F.

2. Arrange the wings in a baking pan so that they are not touching.

3. Combine the oil and garlic, and spoon the mixture over the wings. Make sure you get a little of the crushed garlic on each piece.

4. Sprinkle the wings with salt and pepper to taste, and then with enough paprika to make them reddish allover.

5. Roast for 15 to 20 minutes, then turn them over and sprinkle the other side with salt, pepper, and paprika.

6. Roast for another 45 minutes to 1 hour, turning every 15 to 20 minutes.

Yield: 20 pieces, each with a trace of carbohydrates, a trace of fiber, and 4 grams of protein.

Stuffed Eggs

Don't save these recipes for parties: If you're a low-carb eater, a refrigerator full of stuffed eggs is a beautiful thing. Here are six varieties. Feel free to double or triple any of these recipes-you know they'll disappear.

Classic Deviled Eggs

These are everybody's potluck supper favorite.

6 hard-boiled eggs
5 tablespoons mayonnaise

2 teaspoons spicy brown or Dijon mustard 1/4 teaspoon salt or
Vege-Sal
Paprika

1. Slice the eggs in half, and carefully remove the yolks into a mixing bowl.

2. Mash the yolks with a fork. Stir in the mayonnaise, mustard, and salt, and mix until creamy.

3. Spoon the mixture back into the hollows in the egg whites. Sprinkle with a little paprika for color.

Yield: 12 halves, each with a trace of carbohydrates, a trace of fiber, and 3 grams of protein.

Onion Eggs

6 hard-boiled eggs
5 tablespoons mayonnaise
1 teaspoon spicy brown or Dijon mustard

2 1/2 teaspoons very finely minced sweet red onion 5 drops Tabasco
1/4 teaspoon salt or Vege-Sal

Slice the eggs in half, and carefully remove the yolks into a mixing bowl.

Mash the yolks with a fork. Stir in the mayonnaise, mustard, onion, Tabasco, and salt, and mix until creamy.

Spoon the mixture back into the hollows in the egg whites.

Yield: 12 ha Ives, each with a trace of ca rbohyd rates, a trace of fi ber, and 3 grams of protein.

Fish Eggs

That's eggs with fish, not eggs from fish. If you thought stuffed eggs couldn't go to an upscale party, these will change your mind.

6 hard-boiled eggs
2 tablespoons mayonnaise
2 tablespoons sour cream
1/4 cup moist smoked salmon, mashed fine 1 tablespoon jarred, grated horseradish
2 teaspoons finely minced sweet red onion 1/8 teaspoon salt

1. Slice the eggs in half, and carefully remove the yolks into a mixing bowl.

2. Mash the yolks with a fork. Stir in the mayonnaise, sour cream, salmon, horseradish, onion, and salt, and mix until creamy.

3. Spoon the mixture back into the hollows in the egg whites.

Yield: 12 halves, each with a trace of carbohydrates, a trace of fiber, and 3 grams of protein.

Kali's Eggs

Curried and buttery and good!

6 hard-boiled eggs
1 tablespoon butter
1 teaspoon curry powder
1 clove garlic, crushed
1 scallion, including the crisp part of the green shoot, finely minced 1/3 cup mayonnaise
1/4 teaspoon Tabasco
1/2 teaspoon salt

1.   Slice the eggs in half, and carefully remove the yolks into a mixing bowl.

2.   In a small, heavy skillet over low heat, melt the butter. Add the curry powder and garlic, and stir for 2 minutes.

3.   Scrape the butter mixture into the yolks. Stir in the scallion, mayonnaise, Tabasco, and salt, and mix until creamy.

4. Spoon the mixture back into the hollows in the egg whites.

Yield: 12 halves, each with 1 gram of carbohydrates, a trace of fiber, and 3 grams of protein.

Hammond Eggs

Deviled ham gives these eggs a country sort of kick.

6 hard-boiled eggs
1 can (2 1/4 ounces) of deviled ham 4 teaspoons spicy brown
mustard 3 tablespoons mayonnaise
1/4 teaspoon salt
Paprika

Slice the eggs in half, and carefully remove the yolks into a
mixing bowl.

Mash the yolks with a fork. Stir in the ham, mustard,
mayonnaise, and salt, and mix until creamy.

Spoon the mixture back into the hollows in the egg whites.
Sprinkle with a little paprika for color.

Yield: Makes 12 halves, each with 1 gram of carbohydrates, a
trace of fiber, and 4 grams of protein .

Cajun Eggs

6 hard-boiled eggs
1/3 cup mayonnaise
2 teaspoons horseradish mustard
1 teaspoon Cajun Seasoning

1. Slice the eggs in half, and carefully remove the yolks into a mixing bowl.

2. Mash the yolks with a fork. Stir in the mayonnaise and mustard, and mix until

creamy.

3. Add the Cajun seasoning, and blend well.

4. Spoon the mixture back into the hollows in the egg whites.

Yield: 12 halves, each with 1 gram of carbohydrates, a trace of fiber, and 3 grams of protein.

Artichoke Parmesan Dip

Serve this party favorite with pepper strips, cucumber rounds, celery

sticks, or low-carb fiber crackers.

1 can (13 1/2 ounces) artichoke hearts
1 cup mayonnaise
1 cup grated Parmesan cheese
1 clove garlic, crushed, or 1 teaspoon of jarred, chopped garlic
Paprika

1. Preheat the oven to 325°F.

2. Drain and chop the artichoke hearts.

3. Mix the artichoke hearts with the mayonnaise, cheese, and garlic, combining well.

4. Put the mixture in a small, oven-proof casserole, sprinkle a little paprika on top, and bake for 45 minutes.

Yield: 4 servings, each with 3 grams of carbohydrates and 1 gram of fiber, for a total of 2 grams of usable carbs and 10 grams of protein.

Spinach Artichoke Dip

This is a great, equally yummy version of the previous recipe, but keep

in mind that it does make twice as much dip.

1 can (13 1/2 ounces) artichoke hearts
1 package frozen chopped spinach (10 ounces), thawed
2 cups mayonnaise
2 cups grated Parmesan cheese
2 cloves garlic, crushed, or 2 teaspoons jarred, chopped garlic
Paprika

1. Drain and chop the artichoke hearts.

2. Combine the spinach, mayonnaise, cheese, and garlic in a large casserole

(a 6-cup dish is about right) . Sprinkle with paprika.

3. Bake at 325°F for 50 to 60 minutes.

Yield: 8 servings, each with 4 grams of carbohydrates and 2 grams of fiber, for a total of 2 grams of usable carbs and 10 grams of protein.

Guacamole

This is a very simple guacamole recipe, without sour cream or mayonnaise, that lets the taste of the avocados shine through.

4 ripe black avocados
2 tablespoons minced sweet red onion 3 tablespoons lime juice
3 cloves garlic, crushed
1/4 teaspoon Tabasco
Salt or Vege-Sal to taste

1. Halve the avocados, and scoop the flesh into a mixing bowl. Mash coarsely with a fork.

2. Mix in the onion, lime juice, garlic, Tabasco, and salt, stirring to blend well and mashing to the desired consistency.

Yield: 6 generous servings, each with 11 grams of carbohydrates and 3 grams of fiber, for a total of 8 grams of usable carbs and 3 grams of protein.

This recipe contains lots of healthy fats and almost three times the potassium found in a banana.

DiII Dip

This easy dip tastes wonderful with all sorts of raw vegetables; try serving it with celery, peppers, cucumber, broccoli, or whatever else you have on hand.

1 pint sour cream
1/4 small onion
1 heaping tablespoon dry dill weed 1/2 teaspoon salt or Vege-Sal

1. Put the sour cream, onion, dill weed, and salt in a food processor, and process until the onion disappears. (If you don't have a food processor, mince the onion very fine and just stir everything together.)

2. You can serve this right away, but it tastes even better if you let it chill for a few hours.

Yield: 1 pint, containing 25 grams of carbohydrates and 1 gram of fiber, for a total
of 24 grams of usable carbs and 16 grams of protein in the batch. (This is easily enough for 10 to 12 people, so no one's going to get more than a few grams of carbs.)

Clam Dip

With some celery sticks and pepper strips for scooping, this would make a good lunch. Of course you can serve it at parties, too, with celery, green pepper, cucumber rounds, or fiber crackers for you and crackers or chips for the non low-carbers.

2 packages (8 ounces each) cream cheese, softened 1/2 cup mayonnaise
2 to 3 teaspoons Worcestershire sauce
1 tablespoon Dijon mustard

8 to 10 scallions, including the crisp part of the green shoot, minced 2 cans (6 1/2 ounces each) minced clams, drained
Salt or Vege-Sal

Pepper

Combine all the ingredients well, and chill. A food processor or blender works well for this, or if you prefer to leave chunks of clam, you could use an electric mixer.

Yield: 12 servings, each with just under 4 grams of carbohydrates, a trace of fiber, and 10 grams of protein.

Northwest Dip

Low carbezine! reader Pat Moriarty says, "This is my all-time favorite!"

1 package (8 ounces) cream cheese, softened 1/4 cup heavy cream
1 green onion, thinly sliced
2 teaspoons freshly squeezed lemon juice

1 dash red pepper sauce
4 ounces smoked salmon, gently shredded 1 ripe avocado, mashed

1. In a large mixing bowl, combine the cream cheese and heavy cream together until smooth and creamy.

2. Stir in the onion, lemon juice, and red pepper sauce. Gently fold in the smoked salmon and mashed avocado, being careful not to over-mix.

3. Serve with cucumber, celery, your choice of low-carb crackers, or pork rinds. *Yield:* 6 servings, each with 4 grams of carbohydrates and 1 gram of fiber,

for a total of 3 grams of usable carbs and 7 grams of protein.

Kathy's Pork Rind Dip

When she gets tired of eating plain pork rinds, *Lowcarbezine!* reader

Kathy Rice makes this dip to go with them.

3 ounces cream cheese, softened 2 tablespoons salsa

Blend and enjoy-that's all there is to it.

Yield: 2 servings, each with 2 grams of carbohydrates and 0.5 gram of fiber, for a total of 1.5 grams of usable carbs and 3.5 grams of protein.

Avocado Cheese Dip

This dip has been known to make my mom a very popular person at parties. Dip with pork rinds, vegetables, or purchased protein chips. It can also be served over steak, and it makes perhaps the most elegant omelets on the face of the earth.

2 packages (8 ounces each) cream cheese, softened
1 1/2 cups shredded white Cheddar or Monterey jack cheese
1 ripe black avocado, peeled and seeded
1 small onion
1 clove garlic, crushed
1 can (3 to 4 ounces) green chilies, drained, or jalapenos, if you like it hot

1. Combine all the ingredients in a food processor, and process until very smooth. 2. Scrape into a pretty serving bowl, and place the avocado seed in the middle.

For some reason, placing the seed in the middle keeps the dip from turning brown quite so quickly while it sits out. But if you're making this a few hours ahead of time, cover it with plastic wrap, making sure the wrap is actually

touching the surface of the dip. Don't make this more than a few hours before you plan to serve it.

Yield: About 5 cups (plenty for a good-size party), with the batch containing 45 grams of carbohydrates and 9 grams of fiber, for a total of 36 grams of usable carbs and a whopping 83 grams of protein.

Smoked Gouda Veggie Dip

Great with celery, peppers, or any favorite raw veggie.
Combine your ingredients with a mixer, not a food processor,
so you have actual little bits of Gouda in the dip.

1 package (8 ounces) cream cheese, softened
2/3 cup mayonnaise
1 cup shredded smoked Gouda
6 scallions, including the crisp part of the green shoot, sliced 2
tablespoons grated Parmesan cheese

1/2 teaspoon pepper
1. Beat the cream cheese and mayonnaise together until
creamy, scraping the sides

of the bowl often.
2. Add the Gouda, scallions, Parmesan, and pepper, and beat
until well blended. 3. Chill, and serve with raw vegetables.

Yield: At least 8 servings, each with 2 grams of carbohydrates,
a trace of fiber, and 7 grams of protein.

Kim's Crab Dip

We have my sister to thank for coming up with this delicious, low-carb

treat.

1 package (8 ounces) cream cheese, softened 1/2 cup sour cream
1 can (6 ounces) crabmeat, drained
1 teaspoon horseradish

2 tablespoons fresh chives, or dried if fresh are unavailable 1/4 teaspoon dry mustard
1/8 teaspoon salt
1/8 teaspoon pepper

1. Beat the cheese and sour cream together at a high speed until very smooth.
2. Set the beater to a low speed, and mix in the crab, horseradish, chives, mustard,

salt, and pepper.
3. Chill. Serve with raw vegetables.

Yield: 12 servings, each containing 1 gram of carbohydrates, a trace of fiber, and 5 grams of protein.

Bacon Cheese Spread

Another recipe from Jen Eloff's *Splendid Low-Carbing*. Jen, of

sweety.com, says, "Your friends will beg you for this recipe!"

1 package (8 ounces) light cream cheese, softened 1/2 cup mayonnaise
1 1/2 cups shredded Cheddar cheese
2 tablespoons chopped fresh chives or scallions

1 teaspoon dried parsley
1/4 teaspoon garlic powder
8 slices bacon, cooked until crisp

1.   Preheat the oven to 350°F.

2.   In a food processor with the S blade in place or in a blender, process the cream cheese and mayonnaise until smooth.

3.   In a medium bowl, combine the cream cheese mixture, Cheddar, chives, parsley, and garlic powder until well combined. Spread the mixture evenly on the bottom of a 9-inch glass pie plate.

4.   Use a pair of kitchen scissors to cut the cooked bacon into small pieces. Garnish the top of the cheese spread with the bacon pieces, and bake for 15 minutes. Serve with

low-carb crackers.

Yield: 12 servings, each with 2 grams of carbohydrates, a trace of fiber, and 7 grams of protein.

—

Dukkah

My friend Lou Anne brought this Turkish "dry dip" along on a campout, and I've been nagging her for the recipe ever since. Although Dukkah is traditionally eaten with bread, it also adds an exotic, fascinating flavor to simple raw vegetables.

1/3 cup almonds or hazelnuts 1/4 cup white sesame seeds 1/4 cup coriander seeds
1/4 cup cumin seeds

Salt and pepper to taste

1. Toast the nuts, sesame seeds, coriander seeds, and cumin seeds over high heat for 1 minute, stirring constantly.

2. Use a food processor, coffee grinder, or mortar and pestle to crush the toasted mix- ture, then season it with salt and pepper. (Don't over-grind; you want a consistency similar to coarse-ground cornmeal.)

3. Put your Dukkah in a bowl next to a bowl of olive oil, and set out cut-up raw vegetables. Dip the vegetables first into the oil, then into the Dukkah, and eat.

Yield: Just over a cup or about 10 servings, each with 4 grams of carbohydrates and 1 gram of fiber, for a total of 3 grams of usable carbs and. 2 grams of protein . (Analysis does not include vegetables.)

Tuna Pate

If you throw in some veggies for dipping, this versatile dish makes a great snack, first course at a dinner party, or even a fine brown bag lunch.

2 tablespoons butter
2 cloves garlic, crushed
1/2 medium onion, chopped
1 can (4 ounces) mushrooms, drained
1/2 teaspoon orange extract
1 tablespoon Splenda
1 package (8 ounces) cream cheese, softened 1 can (6 ounces) tuna, drained
2 tablespoons fresh parsley
Grated rind of half an orange
1/4 teaspoon salt
1/4 teaspoon pepper

1. In a small, heavy skillet over medium heat, melt the butter and saute the garlic, onion, and mushrooms until the onion is limp. Add the orange extract and Splenda, and stir well. Cool.

2. Place the cream cheese, tuna, parsley, orange rind, salt, and pepper in a food processor with the Sblade in place. Pulse to blend. Add the sauteed mixture, and pulse until smooth and well blended.

3. Spoon into a serving bowl and chill. Serve with celery sticks, pepper strips, cucumber rounds, and crackers (for the carb-eaters).

Yield: At least 6 servings, each with 3 grams of carbohydrates and1 gram of fiber, for a total of 2 grams of usable carbs and 11 grams of protein.

Marinated Mushrooms

The quality of the vinaigrette dressing makes all the difference here, so

use the best you can make or buy.

8 ounces small, fresh mushrooms
1 1/2 cups vinaigrette dressing (homemade or store-bought)

1. Thoroughly wipe the mushrooms clean with a soft cloth.

2. Place them in a saucepan, cover them with the dressing, and simmer over a medi- um low burner for 15 minutes.

3. Chill and drain the mushrooms, saving the dressing to store any leftover mushrooms in. (You can even simmer another batch of mushrooms in it when the first batch is gone.) Arrange the mushrooms on lettuce with toothpicks for spearing.

Yield: Depending on the size of your mushrooms, this will make about 12 to 15 serv- ings, each with about 1 gram of carbohydrates and not enough fiber or protein to talk about.

Cheese Cookies

This recipe requires a food processor, so if you only have a tiny one, cut the recipe in half. Despite the name, these are not sweet; they're more like cheese crackers.

1/2 pound processed American loaf cheese, like Velveeta (store brand works fine)

1/2 pound sharp Cheddar cheese
1/4 pound butter
1 cup soy powder
About 6 dozen pecan or walnut halves (optional)

1. Preheat the oven to 400°F.

2. Cut the loaf cheese, Cheddar, and butter into chunks.

3. Put the cheese chunks, butter, and soy powder in the food processor, and pulse until the dough is well combined.

4. Coat a cookie sheet with nonstick cooking spray. Drop spoonfuls of dough onto the cookie sheet, and press half a pecan or walnut in the top of each one (if using).

5. Bake for 8 to 10 minutes, or until the cookies are just getting brown around the edges.

Yield: This will depend on how big you make your cookies. I make mine small and get 6 dozen, each with 1 gram of carbohydrates, a trace of fiber, and 2 grams of protein.

Snaps

Similar to the Cheese Cookies on previous page, but these bite back!

1 pound processed jalepeno Jack cheese 1/4 pound butter
1 cu p soy powder

1. Preheat the oven to 400°F.

2. Cut the cheese and butter into chunks.

3. Put the cheese, butter, and soy powder in the food processor, and pulse until the dough is well combined.

4. Coat a cookie sheet with nonstick cooking spray. Drop spoonfuls of dough onto the cookie sheet.

5. Bake for 8 to 10 minutes, or until the cookies are just getting brown around the edges.

Yield: This will depend on how big you make your cookies. I make mine small, and get 6 dozen, each with 1 gram of carbohydrates, a trace of fiber, and 2 grams of protein.

Roasted Nuts

Of course you can buy these in a can at the grocery store, but they're

much better-and cheaper-when you roast them fresh at home.

2 cups shelled nuts of your choice (almonds, pecans, walnuts, or a combination) 4 tablespoons butter, melted
Salt

Preheat the oven to 300°F.
Spread the nuts in a shallow roasting pan. Stir in the butter, coating all the nuts. Roast for 20 to 25 minutes. Remove from the oven and salt to taste.

Yield: 8 servings. Each serving made with almonds will have 7 grams of carbohydrates and 4 grams of fiber, for a total of 3 grams of usable carbs and 7 grams of protein. Each serving made with pecans will have 5 grams of carbohydrates and 2 grams of

fiber, for a total of 3 grams of usable carbs and 2 grams of protein. Each serving made with walnuts will have 5 grams of carbohydrates and 1 gram of fiber, for a total of 4 grams of usable carbs and 4 grams of protein .

Soy and Ginger Pecans

I gave away tins of these for Christmas one year and got rave
reviews.

2 cups shelled pecans
4 tablespoons butter, melted 3 tablespoons soy sauce
1 teaspoon ground ginger

1. Preheat the oven to 300°F.

2. Spread the pecans in a shallow roasting pan. Stir in the
    butter, coating all the nuts.

3. Roast for 15 minutes, then remove from the oven and
    stir in the soy sauce. Sprinkle the ginger evenly over the
    nuts, and stir that in as well.

4. Roast for another 10 minutes.

Yield: 8 servings, each with 6 grams of carbohydrates
and 2 grams of fiber, for a total of 4 grams of usable
carbs and 3 grams of protein.

Worcestershire Nuts

I like to use this combination of nuts, but feel free to use just one or

the other, or to experiment with your own proportions.

1 cup shelled walnuts
1 cup shelled pecans
4 tablespoons butter, melted
3 tablespoons Worcestershire sauce

1. Preheat the oven to 300°F.

2. Spread the nuts in a shallow baking pan, and stir in the butter, coating all the nuts.

3. Roast for 15 minutes, then remove from the oven and stir in the Worcestershire sauce.

4. Roast for another 10 minutes.

Yield: 8 servings, each with 6 grams of carbohydrates and 2 grams of fiber, for a total of 4 grams of usable carbs and 3 grams of protein.

Curried Pecans

When I first came up with this combination of seasonings, I intended to use it on chicken, but I've discovered that it's also delicious on pecans.

2 cups shelled pecans
4 tablespoons butter, melted
1 tablespoon Chicken Seasoning (see page 404)

1. Preheat the oven to 300°F.
2. Spread the nuts in a shallow baking pan, and stir in the butter, coating all the nuts.

3. Roast for 20 to 25 minutes.

4. Remove from the oven, sprinkle Chicken Seasoning over the nuts, and stir to coat.

Yield: 8 servings, each with 5 grams of carbohydrates and 2 grams of fiber, for a total of 3 grams of usable carbs and 2 grams of protein.

Dana's SnackMix

You can buy shelled sunflower seeds and pumpkin seeds in bulk at most health food stores, and you should be able to get raw cashew pieces there, too. For variety, try adding 2 1/2 cups of low-carb garlic croutons along with the seeds and nuts.

6 tablespoons butter
3 tablespoons Worcestershire sauce
1 1/2 teaspoons garlic powder
2 1/2 teaspoons seasoned salt
1 teaspoon onion powder
2 1/2 cups raw, shelled sunflower seeds 2 1/2 cups raw, shelled pumpkin seeds 1 cup almonds
1 cup pecans
1 cup walnuts
1 cup raw cashew pieces

1. Preheat the oven to 250°F.

2. In a small pan, melt the butter and stir in the Worcestershire sauce, garlic powder, seasoned salt, and onion powder.

3. In a large bowl, combine the seeds and nuts. Pour the melted butter mixture over them, and mix very well.

4. Put the mixture in large roasting pan, and bake for 2 hours, stirring occasionally.

5. Allow the mixture to cool, and store in an airtight container.

Yield: 18 servings, each with 14 grams of carbohydrates and 5 grams of fiber, for a total of 9 grams of usable carbs and 13 grams of protein.

RanchMix

2 cups raw, shelled pumpkin seeds 2 cups raw, shelled
sunflower seeds 2 cups dry-roasted peanuts
1 cup raw almonds

1 cu p raw cashew pieces
2 tablespoons canola oil
1 packet dry ranch salad dressing mix 1 teaspoon lemon
pepper
1 teaspoon dried dill
1/2 teaspoon garlic powder

1. Preheat the oven to 350°F.

2. In large mixing bowl, combine the pumpkin seeds,
sunflower seeds, peanuts, almonds, and cashews. Add the
canola oil, and stir to coat. Add the dressing mix,

lemon pepper, dill, and garlic powder, and stir until well
distributed.

3. Put the seasoned nuts in shallow roasting pan, and roast for
45 to 60 minutes, stirring occasionally, until the almonds are
crisp through.

Yield: 16 servings, each with 15 grams of carbohydrates and 5
grams of fiber, for a total of 10 grams of usable carbs and 16
grams of protein.

Asian Punks

Pumpkin seeds are terrific for you-they're a great source of both magnesium and zinc.

And they taste great, too.

2 cups raw, shelled pumpkin seeds 2 tablespoons soy sauce
1/2 teaspoon powdered ginger
2 teaspoons Splenda

1. Preheat the oven to 350°F.

2. In a mixing bowl, combine the pumpkin seeds, soy sauce, ginger, and Splenda, mixing well.

3. Spread the pumpkin seeds in a shallow roasting pan, and roast for about 45 minutes,

or until the seeds are dry, stirring two or three times during roasting.

Yield: 4 servings, each with 13 grams of carbohydrates and 3 grams of fiber, for a total of 10 grams of usable carbs and 17 grams of protein. (These are also a terrific source of minerals.)

Indian Punks

You can actually buy curry-flavored pumpkin seeds, but these are bet- ter tasting and better for you.

4 tablespoons butter
2 1/2 tablespoons curry powder
2 cloves garlic, crushed
2 cups raw, shelled pumpkin seeds Salt

1. Preheat the oven to 300°F.

2. Melt the butter in a small skillet over medium heat. Add the curry and garlic, and stir for 2 to 3 minutes.

3. In a mixing bowl, add the seasoned butter to the pumpkin seeds, and stir until well coated .

4. Spread the pumpkin seeds in a shallow roasting pan and roast for 30 minutes. Sprinkle lightly with salt.

Yield: 4 servings, each with 15 grams of carbohydrates and 4 grams of fiber, for a total of 11 grams of usable carbs and 18 grams of protein.

In addition to all the minerals found in the pumpkin seeds, you get the turmeric in the curry powder, which is believed to help prevent cancer.

Punks on the Range

Spicy-chili-crunchy. If you miss barbecue-flavored potato chips, try

snacking on these.

2 cups raw, shelled pumpkin seeds 1 tablespoon canola oil
1 tablespoon chili powder
1 teaspoon salt

Preheat the oven to 350°F.

In a mixing bowl, combine the pumpkin seeds and canola oil, and stir until well coated. Add the chili powder and salt, and stir again.

Spread the seeds in a shallow roasting pan, and roast for about 30 minutes.

Yield: 4 servings, each with 13 grams of carbohydrates and 3 grams of fiber, for a total of 10 grams of usable carbs and 17 grams of protein.

Barbecued Peanuts

1 tablespoon Liquid Smoke flavoring 1 teaspoon
Worcestershire sauce Dash of Tabasco
1/2 cup water

1 1/2 cups dry-roasted peanuts 3 tablespoons butter
Garlic salt

Preheat the oven to 250°F.

In a saucepan, combine the Liquid Smoke, Worcestershire
sauce, Tabasco, and water. Bring to a simmer.

Turn off the heat, and stir in the peanuts. Let the peanuts sit in
the liquid for 30 minutes, stirring occasionally.

Drain off the liquid, and spread the peanuts in a shallow
roasting pan. Bake for at least 1 hour, or until good and dry.
(Stir occasionally to help speed up the process.)

When the peanuts are thoroughly dry, melt the butter and stir
it into the peanuts to coat. Sprinkle lightly with garlic salt.

Yield: 3 servings, each with 16 grams of carbohydrates and 6
grams of fiber, for a total of 10 grams of usable carbs and 17
grams of protein.

Antipasto

This easy dish makes a nice light summer supper. Use some or all of the ingredients listed here, adjusting quantities as necessary.

Wedges of cantaloupe

Salami

Boiled ham

Pepperoncini (mildly hot salad peppers, available in jars near the pickles and olives)

Halved or quartered hard-boiled eggs Marinated mushrooms Black and green olives (get the good ones) Strips of canned pimento

Solid-pack white tuna, drizzled with olive oil Sardines Marinated artichoke hearts (available in cans)

Simply arrange some or all of these things decoratively on a platter, put out a stack of small plates and some forks, and dinner is served.

Yield: Varies with your taste and needs, but here are the basic nutritional breakdowns for the items on your antipasto platter:

Cantaloupe, l/S of a small melon: 4.5 grams of carbohydrates and 0.5 grams of fiber, for a total of 4 grams of usable carbs and 0.5 grams of protein

Salami, 1 average slice: 0.5 grams of carbohydrates, a trace of fiber, and 3 grams of protein

Boiled ham, 1 average slice: a trace of carbohydrates, no fiber, and 3.5 grams of protein

Pepperoncini, 1 average piece: 0.5 grams of carbohydrates, a trace of fiber, and no protein

Hard-boiled eggs, 1/2: 0.3 grams of carbohydrates, no fiber, and 3 grams of protein Marinated mushrooms, 1 average piece: 1 gram of carbohydrates, a trace of fiber,

and no protein
Black olives, 1 large: 0.5 grams of carbohydrates, a trace of fiber, and no protein Green olives, 1 large: a trace of carbohydrates, a trace of fiber, and no protein

Pimento, 1 slice: a trace of carbohydrates, a trace of fiber, and no protein Tuna,3 ounces: no carbohydrates, no fiber, and 22 grams of protein

Sardines,2 average: no carbohydrates, no fiber, and 5 grams of protein (not to mention 91 milligrams of calcium)

Artichoke hearts, 2 quarters: 2 grams of carbohydrates, 1 gram of fiber, and no protein

Maggie's Mushrooms

Lowcarbezine! reader Maggie Cosey sends this recipe.

1 1/2 pounds large mushrooms
20 stuffed green olives
2 packages (8 ounces each) cream cheese, softened 1/8 to 1/4
cup Worcestershire sauce

1.   Preheat the oven to 350°F.

2.   Wash the mushrooms and remove their stems.

3.   Chop the olives by hand or in a food processor.

4.   In a mixing bowl, combine the olives, cream cheese, and
Worcestershire sauce.
(Be careful with the Worcestershire; there's a fine line
between not enough and too much, it's better to err on
the side of not enough.)

5.   Spoon the mixture into the mushroom caps, and place
them in a broiler pan.

6.   Bake for 15 to 20 minutes, or until the cream cheese is
slightly browned.

Yield: About 45 mushrooms, each with 1 gram of
carbohydrates, a trace of fiber, and 1 gram of protein.

Simple Low-Carb Stuffed Mushrooms

Lowcarbezine! reader Kayann Kretschmar says, "My Christmas Eve

guests raved about them!"

1 pound medium mushrooms

1 pound bulk breakfast sausage, hot or sage

1 package (8 ounces) cream cheese Preheat the oven to 350°F.

Clean the mushrooms. Remove their stems and use a paring knife to make the hole for stuffing larger.

Q Waste not, want not: If you freeze those stems and mushroom insides, you can use them for sauteed mushrooms the next time you have steak.

Brown and drain the sausage, and stir in the cream cheese. Spoon the mixture into the mushroom caps.

Bake for 20 minutes.

Yield: About 30 mushrooms, each with 1 gram of carbohydrates, a trace of fiber, and 3 grams of protein.

Kay's Crab-Stuffed Mushrooms

These are for my cyberpal Kay, who repeatedly begged me to come up with a low-carb recipe for crab puffs. I tried and tried, but all my attempts were relatively pathetic. So I made crab-stuffed mushrooms instead, and they were a big hit.

1 pound fresh mushrooms
1 can (6 1/2 ounces) flaked crab
2 ounces cream cheese
1/4 cup mayonnaise
1/4 cup grated Parmesan cheese
10 to 12 scallions, including the crisp part of the green shoot, finely sliced Dash of Tabasco
1/4 teaspoon pepper

1. Preheat the oven to 325°F.

2. Wipe the mushrooms clean with a damp cloth, and remove their stems.

3. In a good-size bowl, combine the crab, cream cheese, mayonnaise, parmesan, scal- lions, Tabasco, and pepper well.

4. Spoon the mixture into the mushroom caps, and arrange them in a large, flat roasting pan.

5.

Bake for 45 minutes to 1 hour, or until the mushrooms are done through. Serve hot (although folks will still scarf 'em down after they cool off).

Yield: 25 to 30 mushrooms, each with 1 gram of carbohydrates, a trace of fiber, and 3 grams of protein.

Q Warning: You may be tempted to make these with "fake crab" to save money. Don't. That stuff has a ton of carbohydrates added. Spend the extra couple of bucks and use real crab.

Vicki's Crab-Stuffed Mushrooms

Another tempter from Vicki Cash's 2002 *Low Carb Success Calendar!*

10 ounces medium portobello mushrooms 2 Wasa Fi ber Rye crackers
1 can (6 ounces) crabmeat
1 egg

2 tablespoons lemon juice
1 tablespoon dried dill weed
1 teaspoon dehydrated onion flakes 1/2 cup grated Parmesan cheese

1. Preheat the oven to 400°F.

2. Wipe the mushrooms clean with a damp cloth, and remove their stems. Set aside 1/2 cup of stems. Place the caps on an ungreased baking sheet.

3. Use a food processor with the S blade attached to grind the crackers into coarse crumbs. Add the 1/2 cup of mushroom stems, processing until coarsely chopped. Add the crabmeat, egg, lemon juice, dill, onion, and cheese. Mix thoroughly.

4. Spoon the mixture into the mushroom caps and bake for 12 to 15 minutes, or until the top of the stuffing is slightly browned. Serve hot.

Yield: 6 appetizer-size servings, each with 4.5 grams of carbohydrates and 1 gram of fiber, for a total of 3.5 grams of usable carbs and 10 grams of protein.

Two-Cheese Tuna-Stuffed Mushrooms

Of all the stuffed mushrooms I've cooked or sampled, these are my

absolute favorites.

1/2 pound fresh mushrooms
1 can tuna
1/2 cup shredded smoked Gouda
2 tablespoons grated Parmesan cheese 3 tablespoons mayonnaise
1 scallion, finely minced

1. Preheat the oven to 350°F.

2. Wipe the mushrooms clean with a damp cloth, and remove their stems.

3. Combine the tuna, Gouda, Parmesan, mayonnaise, and minced scallion, and mix well.

4. Spoon the mixture into the mushroom caps, and arrange them in a shallow roasting pan. Add just enough water to cover the bottom of the pan. Bake for 15 minutes and serve hot.

Yield: About 15 servings, each with 1 gram of carbohydrates, a trace of fiber, and 4 grams of protein.

Turkey-Parmesan Stuffed Mushrooms

1 pound ground turkey
3/4 cup grated Parmesan cheese 1/2 cup mayonnaise
1 teaspoon dried oregano
1 teaspoon dried basil
2 cloves garlic, crushed
1 teaspoon salt or Vege-Sal
1/4 teaspoon pepper
1 1/2 pounds mushrooms

1. Preheat the oven to 350°F.
2. Combine the turkey, Parmesan, mayonnaise, oregano, basil, garlic, salt, and pepper,

mixing very well.

3. Wipe the mushrooms clean with a damp cloth, and remove their stems.

4. Spoon the mixture into the mushroom caps, and place them in a shallow roasting pan. Add just enough water to cover the bottom of the pan. Bake for 20 minutes, and serve hot.

Yield: About 45 mushrooms, each with 1 gram of carbohydrates, a trace of fiber, and 3 grams of protein.

Rumaki

These take a little extra effort, but I think it's worth it because my husband and I both love them.

1/2 cup soy sauce
1/4 cup dry sherry
1 clove garlic, crushed
1 slice fresh gingerroot, about 1/4 inch thick, finely minced 12 strips bacon
12 chicken livers
24 canned whole water chestnuts

1. Mix together the soy sauce, sherry, garlic, and ginger to make the marinade.

2. Cut the bacon strips and chicken livers in half. (You'll find that the livers sort of have two halves naturally.)

3. Wrap each chicken liver half around a water chestnut, then wrap a half-strip of bacon around each chicken liver. Spear the whole thing with a large toothpick or bamboo skewer, making sure you pierce the water chestnut on the way through.

4. Submerge your speared bundles in the marinade, and let them marinate for at least an hour. (You can let them marinate overnight, if you want to prepare this dish well in advance of your company arriving.)

5. When you're ready to eat, take the bundles out of the marinade and broil or grill them for 5 to 7 minutes on each side, until the bacon is crisp.

Yield: Makes 24. When I analyzed this recipe, it came up with 10 grams of carbohy- drates per piece, but the software was assuming that you consume all of the mari- nade, which of course you do not. These should

---

actually have about 3 grams of car- bohydrates apiece and 1 gram of fiber, for a total of about 2 grams of usable carbs and 5 grams of protein-pius all of the nutrients liver is famous for.

If you like, you may leave the water chestnuts out of these, and the carb count will drop to a mere trace.

Country-Style Pate

This is really good. Plus, as pate goes, it's easy to make.

6 slices bacon
2 tablespoons butter
1 cup sliced mushrooms
1/2 cup chopped onion
1 cup chicken livers
1/2 teaspoon Worcestershire sauce 2 tablespoons mayonnaise
Scant 1/2 teaspoon salt or Vege-Sal 1/4 teaspoon pepper

In a heavy skillet over medium heat, fry the bacon until it just starts to get crisp. Remove the bacon, and drain and reserve the grease.

Turn the burner down to low, and melt the butter and a little bacon grease in the skillet. Saute the mushrooms and onion in the skillet until they're quite limp (about 15 minutes).

While they're sauteing, fill a medium saucepan with water, and bring it to a boil. Put the chicken livers in the water (make sure you keep stirring those sauteing

vegetables), and bring the water back to a boil. Cover the pan, turn off burner, and let it sit for 15 minutes.

Drain the chicken livers. Put them in a food processor with the S blade in place and pulse two or three times to grind the chicken livers. Crumble and add the bacon and

the mushroom and onion mixture. Pulse to combine. Add the Worcestershire, may- onnaise, salt, and pepper, and pulse again, until well combined. Serve with celery sticks, pepper strips, or low-carb crackers.

Yield: 12 servings, each with 2 grams of carbohydrates, a trace of fiber, and 5 grams of protein.

Christmas Liver Pate

Lowcarbezine! reader Elizabeth Czilok sends this recipe, and says, "It's cute, Christmassy, yummy, and low-carb." Save it for Christmas if you like, but my recipe tester insists it's good any time, and on nearly anything.

8 ounces liverwurst (use the best you can find) 1 package (8 ounces) cream cheese, softened 1/3 cup finely chopped onion 2 to 3 tablespoons sour cream

1/2 teaspoon Worcestershire sauce
1/4 teaspoon hot pepper sauce (optional) Stuffed olives to garnish

1. Mix the liverwurst, half the cream cheese, the onion, sour cream, Worcestershire sauce, and hot pepper sauce, combining well.

2. Form a mound of pate in the center of a serving dish. Place the dish and pate in the freezer for about 15 minutes.

3. Frost with the remaining softened cream cheese.

4. Slice a few green olives stuffed with pimentos so the green is a circle on the outside with the red pimento on the inside. Arrange them on the outside of the mound as a garnish, and serve with low-carb crackers and veggies.

Yield: Just over a pound of pate, or 16 servings, each with 1 gram of carbohydrates, almost no fiber, and 3 grams of protein. Four stuffed olives contain about 3 grams of carbohydrates, very little fiber, and no protein.

Celery Stuffed with Bleu Cheese and Cream Cheese.

Lowcarbezine! reader Jeannette Regas sends this easy low-carb crowd-pleaser.

5 or 6 large ribs of celery
1/4 cup crumbled bleu cheese, at room temperature
1 package (8 ounces) cream cheese, at room temperature
Heavy cream (optional)
Salt and pepper

1. Clean the ribs of celery, and cut them into 3- to 4-inch pieces.

2. Mix the crumbled bleu cheese with the cream cheese, adding a little cream to make it smooth, if necessary. Add a little salt and pepper to taste.

3. Stuff into celery, and serve.

Yield: 15 to 18 pieces, each with 1 gram of carbohydrates, a trace of fiber, and 2 grams of protein.

Fried Cheese

This is the sort of decadence I would never have considered in my low-fat days.

If you miss cheese-flavored snacks, you've got to try this. 2 or 3 tablespoons olive or canola oil

1/2 to 3/4 cup shredded Cheddar, Monterey Jack, or jalepeno Jack cheese

1. Spray a small, heavy bottomed, nonstick skillet with nonstick cooking spray, and place

   over medium-high heat.

2. Add the oil, and then the cheese. The cheese will melt and bubble and spread to fill the bottom of the skillet.

3. Let the cheese fry until it's crisp and brown around the edges. Use a spatula to lift up an edge, and check whether the cheese is brown all over the bottom; if it isn't, let it go another minute or so.

4. When the fried cheese is good and brown, carefully flip it and fry the other side until it, too, is brown.

5. Remove the cheese from the skillet, drain, and lie it flat to cool. Break into pieces and eat.

   Yield: 2 servings, each with 1 gram of carbohydrates, no fiber, and 11 grams of protein.

Cheesy Bowls and Taco Shells. For a tasty, cheesy, tortillalike bowl, follow the directions for Fried Cheese, until you get to Step 5. Then remove and drain the cheese, but drape it over the bottom of a bowl to cool. When it cools and hard- ens, you'll have a cheesy, edible bowl to eat a taco salad out of.

You can also make a taco shell by folding the cheese disc in half and propping it partway open. Be careful when handling it, though; hot cheese can burn you pretty seriously.

Saganaki

If you've never tried the Greek cheese Kasseri, you're in for a treat. This dish is fantastically delicious, and has a dramatic, fiery presentation to boot.

1/4 pound Kasseri, in a slab 1/2 inch thick
1 egg, beaten
2 to 3 tablespoons rice protein powder, soy powder, or low-carb bake mix Olive oil
1 shot brandy
1/4 lemon

1. Dip the slab of cheese in the beaten egg, then in the protein powder, coating it all over.

2. Heat 1/4 inch of olive oil in a heavy skillet over medium heat. When the oil is hot, add the cheese.

3. Fry until golden and crisp on both sides, turning only once. Remove from the pan and put on a fire-proof plate.

4. Pour the brandy evenly over the hot cheese, strike a match, and light the brandy on fire. It is traditional to shout "Opa!" at this moment.

5. Squeeze the lemon over the flaming cheese, putting out the fire. Divide in half, and scarf it down!

Yield: 2 servings, each with 3 grams of carbohydrates, a trace of fiber, and 17 grams of protein.

Southwestern Saganaki

A yummy twist on the traditional Saganaki and a perfect starter for a

fiery Mexican dinner for two.

1/4 pound pepper Jack cheese, in a slab 1/2 inch thick
1 egg, beaten
2 to 3 tablespoons rice protein powder, soy powder, or low-carb bake mix Olive oil
1 shot tequila
1/4 lime

1. Dip the slab of cheese in the beaten egg, then in the protein powder, coating it all over.

2. Heat 1/4 inch of olive oil in a heavy skillet over medium heat. When the oil is hot, add the cheese.

3. Fry until golden and crisp on both sides, turning only once. Remove from the pan and put on a fire-proof plate.

4. Pour the tequila evenly over the hot cheese, strike a match, and light the brandy on fire.

S. Squeeze the lime over the flaming cheese, putting out the fire.

Yield: 2 servings, each with 3 grams of carbohydrates, a trace of fiber, and 17 grams of protein.

Pickled Shrimp

This recipe will feed a crowd, so make it when you have plenty of people to share with.

6 cups water
1/4 cup dry sherry
1/2 teaspoon peppercorns
1 bay leaf
6 teaspoons salt
3 pounds raw shrimp, shelled and deveined 1 cup oil
2/3 cup lemon juice
1/2 cup white vinegar
3 tablespoons mixed pickling spice
2 teaspoons Splenda
2 sprigs fresh dill, coarsely chopped

In a large saucepan over high heat, bring the water, sherry, peppercorns, bay leaf, and 2 teaspoons of salt to a boil.

Add the shrimp, and bring back to a boil. Cook 1 minute longer, and drain.

In a large bowl, combine the oil, lemon juice, vinegar, pickling spice, Splenda, dill, and the remaining 4 teaspoons of salt. Add the shrimp, and toss with this pickling mixture.

Cover the bowl, and chill it and the platter you will serve the shrimp on in the refrigerator overnight.

To serve, drain off and discard the marinade, and arrange the shrimp on the platter. Garnish with additional dill, if desired.

~ If it's going to be a long party, it's a good idea to set the platter or bowl on a bed of crushed ice in another container, to keep the shrimp cold.

Yield: This is enough for a party of a few dozen people, but the carb count will differ according to how big your shrimp are, of course! Figure 24 servings, each with less than 1 gram of carbohydrates, a trace of fiber, and 12 grams of protein.

Crab and Bacon Bundles

This quick, hot hors d'oeuvre will impress your guests.

1 can (6 ounces) crab, drained 1 scallion, finely minced
1/2 pound bacon
Duck Sauce (see page 417)

1. Flake the crab, removing any bits of shell or cartilage. Stir in the minced scallion, and set aside.

2. Cut all your bacon strips in half crosswise, to make two shorter strips. Place a round- ed 1/2 teaspoon or so of the crab mixture on the end of a bacon strip, and roll the strip up around it, stretching the bacon slightly as you go. Pierce the bundle with a toothpick, to hold. Repeat until all the crab and bacon strips are used up.

3.

Broil about 8 inches from heat, turning once or twice, until the bacon is crisp-no more than 10 minutes. Serve with Duck Sauce for dipping.

Yield: About 2 dozen servings, each with only a trace of carbohydrates, a trace of fiber, and 4 grams of protein. (Analysis does not include Duck Sauce.)

Conclusion

Thank you again for purchasing this book!
I hope this book was able to help you discover
some amazing Low-Carb recipes. The next step
is to get cooking !!!

Lightning Source UK Ltd.
Milton Keynes UK
UKHW020611231122
412696UK00001B/21

9 781801 822336